KV-374-105

Portraits of

Bath

by John Tompkins

Drawings by Grace D Bratton

Kingsmead

© John Tompkins, Grace D. Bratton, 1976, 1983, 1986

Kingsmead Press
Annesley House
21 Southside
Weston-super-Mare
Avon BS23 2QU

ISBN 0 901571 80 6

Printed in Great Britain at The Bath Press, Avon

CONTENTS

THE DREAMING HILLS

When day has fretted through the hours,
and all the sad stupidity of Man
hangs like a cloud
above his proud pretensions to be wise,
let not depression fester in the mind
but turn your thoughts along another path —
Towards the dreaming hills of Bath . . .

To those green sentinels
that cluster round
this happy island in the sea of Time,
whilst all the changing generations pass
over the long-dead Roman grass.
Tread where the legions sought their rest
and left such monuments to mock our pride
that endless wonder is our guide;
and linger too, where Chaucer's bride
set out on her historic ride,
or feel the stir of bygone days
where Georgian Beau and silken gown
still seem to wander through the town.

O dreaming hills, dream on!
and in this timeless city men call Bath
let future generations pause
a thoughtful moment to admire
what God and Man, together, can conspire.

GREAT PULTENEY STREET

Great Pulteney Street . . . the very name
is like the sound of far-off drums,
the slow majestic roll that comes
before a great event . . .

This wide, imposing, avenue of homes
where famous residents,
from Hannah More to William Pitt,[1]
have honoured every stone of it . . .
From Wilberforce to Mrs Thrale,[2]
who tell the fascinating tale
of statesman, novelist and peer
that history has written here.

Would Bulwer Lytton[3] have preferred
to meet Earl Howe?[4] . . . or rather heard
about Napoleon the Third[5] . . .?
Would Sheridan, today, be sure
to meet Miss Linley[6] as before,
although their 'grotto' is no more?

What famous 'shades' might we not meet,
'Taking the air' in Pulteney Street . . .?

FROM BEECHEN CLIFF

One day I stood on Beechen Cliff
above a scene so fair,
it seemed the peace all men desire
might well be waiting there . . .

Protected by the verdant hills,
the winding river ran
through such a graceful city
as was ever built by man.
Stately crescents framed the view,
Georgian terraces and squares
met little courtyards unawares,
and, rising from the busy scene,
the ancient Abbey stood serene . . .

ABBEY GREEN

Old Man Winter knows his worst is done
And, like a tyrant on the run,
turns spiteful in retreat.
Like some doomed dinosaur
he rages through the days
with wind and rain and snow . . .
But soon his blind, frustrated anger
turns to tearful petulance
and, as a sulky child
held back from seeking to destroy
another's toy,
slinks weeping to the swirling skirts of March.

And then the first, fair messengers of Spring
raise eager heads toward the fitful sun
and, one by one,
the brave, shy, snowdrops
spread their virgin radiance
from every sheltered nook,
and look toward the longer days
with Nature's own eternal praise.

TRIM BRIDGE (ST JOHN'S GATE)

The ghosts of bygone days still linger here,
What memories of yesteryear come crowding back
beneath this ancient arch?

Was it not General Wolfe at Number 5[1]
who waited for his fateful call to take Quebec . . .?
Was it not here at Barton House
that William Sherston, first Lord Mayor of Bath,[2]
would entertain the Queen,
who gave the City Charter
in Elizabethan days?
Did not the 'tall house' once belong
to those enchanting 'pretty milliners' of Bath,
The Misses Hoblyn,[3]
who once had spread their scarlet cloth
to grace the entrance for the Duke of York . . .?
And what of that 'Academy of Dance',
made famous by the Misses Fleming[4]
who could say,
'Lord This . . . or Lady That . . .
if you desire to stay,
you dance *this* way . . .'

And how the very street names,
JOHN and WOOD,[5] recall
the artist-architect who planned
his dream of beauty in an ageless town;
and down the passing years
has left a legacy of gracious days
beyond our praise . . .

Grace D. Bratton

THE ASSEMBLY ROOMS

Beau, Beau,[1]
didn't you know
Lord C. . . . will be at the ball?
No, No, — *NOT* So and So
— *She's* not appearing at all!
They say she is 'resting' just out of the town
— Could be at Batheaston[2] . . . or Claverton Down —
Her footman collected a new evening gown
— But *she's* 'resting' just out of the town . . .

Beau, Beau,
didn't you know
the Duchess has sent her regrets?
No, No, — *NOT* what we know
— her gaming is piling up debts!
They say that the Duke almost broke down and wept,
no more I.O.U's will he ever accept.
— I've heard she has threatened to see she is 'kept'
— and we know who will pay all her debts!

Beau, Beau,
didn't you know
some bounder has broken your rules?
No, No, — *NOT* so and so
— Just one of Miss Fanny's[3] young fools!
They say he's suggesting, despite what *you've* said,
you're head over heels (How Wilkes[4] will see red!)
Such lusting for Fanny is almost ill-bred
— Or why should you worry,
in such a deuced hurry,
to bring the fair Murray to bed . . .?

Grace D. Bratton
76

PULTENEY BRIDGE

How many generations lingered here
to watch the swans above the weir?
How many more will pass this way,
dream awhile, and wish to stay?
So, too, beneath a blue Italian sky,
Must Michelangelo have stood
in Florence, sister city gay with flowers,
and watched the Arno long ago
beneath the Ponte Vecchio![1]

Across the bridge the human tide
will eddy where the little shops,
with gay, inviting artistry,
display their tempting wares;
But here the traveller and I
will lean upon the parapet
with Avon drifting by,
to ponder on the sum of things
and wonder why . . .

For is not Time an endless stream,
the bridge our little span?
And who knows all the answers
to the mysteries of Man?

Grace D. Bratton

ROYAL CRESCENT

If you would find
a sense of peace
grown old with time,
and Time itself an island in a quiet sea,
Then come with me
to where the stately homes
of other days
stand proud and dignified
above the town
and seem to drown,
in some strange way,
the clamour of today.

Here will you find a new content,
a fresh perspective to tomorrow's fears,
and all the brooding silence of the bygone years.
The grace, the splendour, and the tears
of human things
will weave a subtle harmony about your ears.
Here will the tattered fragments of your thoughts
steal softly from the smooth, green turf
towards the hill across the way,
ghost upon ghost,
until the angry tumult of the day
is but an echo on a stage;
the rustle of a turning page . . .

THE BATHS OF BATH

Water, water, everywhere
and even some to drink;
Come to the Spa,
dear Grandmama,
it's later than you think!

It's gushing out in gallons
— heaven knows since when —
and I suppose
that heaven knows
just where it goes again!

That doesn't seem a question
for mortals to decide,
— it may, of course,
with equal force,
go rushing back inside!

But one thing *IS* quite certain,
and clearly understood . . .
to take a drink
— to swim *OR* sink —
is bound to do you good!

ΑΡΙΣΤΟΝ ΜΕΝ ΙΔΩΡ

Grace D. Bratton
7/76

THE PUMP ROOM

Come, meet me in the Pump Room
— Doctor Johnson[1] may look by —
Mrs Thrale[2] is back in Pulteney Street
— And Boswell[3] won't say why!

Come, meet me in the Pump Room
— Jane Austen[4] may drop in —
They say her Pride is obvious
— but her Prejudice wears thin!

Come, meet me in the Pump Room
— Lord Y—— and Countess B——
were seen at The Assembly Rooms
— And stayed till nearly three!

Come, meet me at the Pump Room
— Dear lady, if you dare! —
You doubt my gout will let me out . . .?
Good Gad! I'll take a Chair!

GREEN STREET

Here is the fascination of the town,
the hidden corner at the heart of things,
the sudden sense of ages looking down
upon the busy scene . . .
The slim, serenity of spire
above the narrow street;
the small, discreet, selective shops;
the touch of history that stops
the raging torrent of today.

And those who stay to view the church
will find St Michael's is the fourth
custodian of the faith
to stand upon the site . . .
Where parchment scrolls
in Latin or in Chaucer's prose
tell, as each generation shows,
the slow, unfolding, history of Bath;
in careful records of the hopes and fears,
the footprints of six hundred years . . .

National Westminster Bank

Grace D. Bratton

MILSOM STREET

One night I stood in Milsom Street,
Looking down through Milsom Street — silent and alone,
and seemed to hear the sound of hooves
ringing on the stone . . .
Muffled footsteps hurried by
as some fair maiden in her 'chair'
was carried to I know not where.
The cries of link-boys
drifted to my ears
and all the years,
like autumn leaves,
fell silently away;
I felt the throng about me
sway, and heard soft echoes,
laughing, gay;
voices of a bygone day.

In Milsom Street, at Eastertide,
the ladies, in 'full-fashioned-pride',
were on parade;
With powdered wig and dainty shade,
patched and perfumed,
how they made
their elegant approach to town
in Gainsborough garden-party gown . . .

In Milsom Street, at Eastertide,
to Octagon[1] . . . and by my side
I heard the eager voices say,
'Would Gardiner[2] preach?
or would Magee[3] "thunder his divinity"?
— Or maybe, on this special day,
would not Herschel[4] wish to play?'

One day I stood in Milsom Street,
and watched the world go by . . .
Two hundred years have passed away
but who can, with assurance, say
things have changed so much today?

NORTHUMBERLAND PLACE

Amongst the great 'discoveries'
the visitor may find,
there's one delightful memory
he should not leave behind . . .
A secret, friendly, meeting place
— a village in the town —
where all the pressures of today
will seem to slowly melt away.

The gay, enchanting, little shops
will hold him in their spell;
the goods they sell, in colourful array,
with floral decorations,
make a garden all the way.

How rarely will you see a frown
in this quaint corner of the town . . .

Grace D. Bratton
76

LANSDOWN CRESCENT

Here is a setting made for kings,
a 'Mount Olympus' throne,
that Palmer[1] must have known
was fit for Grecian Gods . . .
And yet, for all its majesty,
there is a friendliness
about this happy place;
the Georgian grace
seems interlaced with some warm sense
of neighbours meeting in a village square.

Would not Jane Austen, taking tea
with dear Miss Irvine,[2] sigh to see
her chairmen waiting patiently?
And then, when darkness fell,
not stay beneath the spell
to watch the stars come tumbling down
as link boys moved about the town?

And if, today, we leave the matchless views,
exploring further under Beckford's[3] arch,
how soon we find,
in those intriguing cottages,
so many reasons why we choose
to linger in the mews . . .

Grace D. Bratton
75

SALLY LUNN

Run, run,
Sweet Sally Lunn,
down to the river
with basket and bun.
Spring Gardens[1] are filling,
Parading's begun,
you must not be late —
and you're missing the fun!

Maid, maid,
don't be delayed,
the ferry[2] is waiting
along South Parade.
Your apron is charming,
bewitchingly made,
your wares are delicious —
you'll take *ALL* the trade!

How we can picture you tripping along,
white-covered basket, humming a song . . .
Neat, little, eager, and mob-capped maid,
weaving your way through the gaily-dressed throng.

Run, run,
Sweet Sally Lunn,
Bath *must* discover
it has a new bun;
Soon folk will rally
to Lilliput alley,[3]
they'll *all* come to Sally
— when Dalmer[4] is done!

Grace D. Bratton

THE AMERICAN MUSEUM, CLAVERTON MANOR

From the sheltered lawns of Claverton,
in the setting summer sun,
you catch your breath as you look below
to see the winding Avon flow.
The fabric of a silken dream,
the sunset stream,
wanders on its sylvan way,
unhurried, through the dying day.

The tall trees stand around you in the dusk
in graceful, lonely loveliness;
Across the vale, the green-packed hill
is quiet and still,
and strangely hushed are the woods below,
until
the night is threaded with a silver chord,
and trembling clear is heard
a last, late, bird.

Then, from such peaceful scenes as these,
your thoughts may turn to refugees
in little ships . . . . .
For here above the Manor,
on hills once ruled by Rome,
there flies a friendly banner
--the 'MAYFLOWER'[1] has come home . . .

THE CIRCUS

I came, by moonlight, from Assembly Rooms,
the city sleeping down below;
and, high above, a light on Lansdown —
pendant like a star,
reminded me of battles long ago.
The slow, soft, sound
of footsteps on the time-worn stones,
far off into the night,
shuffled through the silence
like echoes from the past.

In hushed humility
I turned into the vast,
enduring, monument to Georgian Bath
that stands like a majestic crown
upon the town.
Around me stood that final dream
of Wood, the elder, and his son
who finished that great symphony in stone
that would alone
assure the accolade of Time
to fall upon the task his father had begun.

And, suddenly, the names
of Stanhope, Pitt and Gainsborough[1]
were in my mind,
and all the portraits
from his magic brush
that kept so fine a record
for the archives of to-day.
Linley, Sheridan and Lord Clare,[2]
Garrick, Burke[3] and Sterne were there,
Bishop Hurd,[4] Camden and Quinn,
With all the rest came thronging in . . . .

Across the road, upon the green,
the ancient plane trees
whispered in the breeze;
a muted song of long-forgotten things.
And then, unseen,
high in the top-most branches
clear and sweet,
a late bird sings . . .
and all that beauty is complete.

Grace D. Bratton
'78

PARADE GARDENS, SUMMER

Deep is the spell of Summer,
deep as the sea-green tide;
bees on the honeysuckle,
rose for the summer bride . . .

Count not the cost of dreaming,
nor tally the timeless days,
the world has no lighter burden
than the early morning haze.
The wheat in the upland meadow
is a gentle, restless, sea
and the shade of the apple orchard
is a pool of eternity.

Deep is the spell of Summer,
deep as the soul of Man;
Deep as the unknown answer
sought since the world began . . .

NO. 1 ROYAL CRESCENT

Here stood 'young' Wood,
two hundred years ago;
the slow, unwinding of his father's scheme
stretched out before him.
But this, unlike King's Circus,[1]
was his private dream . . .
the first, fair crescent
to his own design.
The sheer simplicity of line,
the proud, majestic, sweep
was all his own;
and yet he must have known
how justly proud
his father would have been
to see this crowning glory
of a Georgian age . . .

And here, today,
how much he would applaud
the careful, tireless efforts to record
the gracious dignity our fathers knew.
Here, too, the visitor may pause
with ample cause to justify his faith
that, even in these restless days,
some still behave as if all life
were not this frenzied, mindless
race from cradle to the grave . . .

Grace D. Bratton
75

CHRISTMAS EVE IN ABBEY CHURCHYARD

The night is full of miracles,
the young, clear, voices fill the square
with fluted cadences;
the midnight bells are rung
and all the air is warm with radiance.
For one long moment
in the hearts of men
tormented Truth is not divisible,
and thoughts unravel in the mind
as if the tangled values of the year
spin slowly clear.

This is the calm, eternal light
that guides the blind stupidity
of human things to smooth, untroubled paths.
Changeless in a changing world
the timeless message is reborn,
the rote of reason or the cynics scorn
no more than ripples on an endless sea;
and still the questing soul of Man
will find no greater benediction
than the shepherd's tale of wondrous things
— immortal manger and the gifts of kings.

INDEX

AGE	POEM	REFERENCE

GREET PULTENEY STREET

1. HANNAH MORE and her four sisters occupied No. 76 Pulteney Street in 1789, then a newly-built house, until 1802. She was a gifted writer and dramatist as well as famous for her 'good works'. Horace Walpole described her as 'Not only one of the cleverest women, but one of the best.' and the Quarterly Review said 'She did as much real good in her generation as any woman that ever held pen.' Her first regular drama, 'The Inflexible Captive' appeared on the Bath stage in 1773. WILLIAM PITT, the elder, Prime Minister and first Earl of Chatham, 'The Great Commoner', occupied No. 70 Pulteney Street as well as, at other times, No. 8 The Circus and 15 Johnstone Street.
2. WILLIAM WILBERFORCE, philanthropist and slave trade abolitionist resided at No. 36 Pulteney Street. MRS THRALE (later Mrs PIOZZI) Samuel Johnson's great friend lived at No. 77.
3. LORD BULWER LYTTON the novelist lived at No. 2.
4. ADMIRAL EARL HOWE lived at No. 71.
5. NAPOLEON, Prince Louis, afterwards Napoleon III lived at No. 55.
6. ELIZABETH LINLEY and RICHARD SHERIDAN, whose marriage was kept secret for some time, only met on rare occasions. One of their favourite, secret, meeting places was the old 'SPRING GARDENS VAUXHALL' pleasure grounds which they reached by means of TOMKINS FERRY BOAT from 'his stairs at the bottom of SOUTH PARADE'. Either together or singly they would go to the grotto in 'Purdie's Gardens' — which once stood beneath the willow tree in what was to become No. 65 Great Pulteney Street.

3 TRIM BRIDGE (ST JOHN'S GATE)

1. GENERAL WOLFE was in residence at No. 5 TRIM STREET when he awaited his call to lead the expedition to capture Quebec.
2. WILLIAM SHERSTON, first Lord Mayor of Bath under Queen Elizabeth's Charter.
3. THE MISSES HOBLYN, the 'pretty milliners' of Bath made their firm in JOHN STREET famous. Their millinery was accepted as the height of fashion after a visit by the Duke and Duchess of York (circa 1795), when a red carpet was laid down the steps at their entrance.
4. THE MISSES FLEMING were the daughters of the eccentric author of 'TIM GINNADRAKE' and a 'HISTORY OF BATH' who lived at No. 7 JOHN STREET. It was here that they set up their famous DANCING ACADEMY which was patronised by all the 'Quality'.
5. JOHN WOOD, the elder (1704—1754).

15	THE ASSEMBLY ROOMS	1. BEAU — RICHARD 'BEAU' NASH, the 'King of Bath', the Georgian Impressario of the Social scene.
		2. BATHEASTON VILLA where poetic festivals were held in Georgian days by LADY MILLER.
		3. FANNY MURRAY reputed to be one of BEAU NASH's conquests among the fair sex, and whose charms also inspired
		4. WILKES to write his famous 'Essay on Women'.
17	PULTENEY BRIDGE	1. PONTE VECCHIO the 'Old Bridge' of FLORENCE, the 'Twin' to PULTENEY BRIDGE, and the only other bridge in Europe to have shops along both sides of its length. PULTENEY BRIDGE was designed by ROBERT ADAM.
23	THE PUMP ROOM	1. DOCTOR SAMUEL JOHNSON, 'the Great Lexicographer' who compiled the first English Dictionary. He came to Bath in 1776 and stayed at THE PELICAN INN in WALCOT STREET. The THREE CUPS was later on the same site.
		2. Mrs THRALE (Later Mrs Piozzi) Dr Johnson's great friend.
		3. JAMES BOSWELL, Dr Johnson's biographer.
		4. JANE AUSTEN frequently stayed with Mr & Mrs Leigh Perrot in No. 1 The Paragon and her family stayed in the house in 1801 and later moved to 4 Sydney Place where they remained for four years. In the autumn of 1804 the family spent some weeks at Lyme Regis but returned to Bath afterwards and moved into apartments at No. 27 Green Park Buildings. It was here that her father the Rev. George Austen died on the 21st January 1805 and was buried in vaults beneath St Swithin's Church, Walcot. The family moved to No. 25 Gay Street for a while before taking up residence towards the end of the year at Southampton.
27	MILSOM STREET	1. THE OCTAGON CHAPEL, opened 1767, was originally a great centre of worship.
		2. The Rev. Dr JOHN GARDINER was a most popular preacher there before his death in 1838.
		3. The Rev. W. C. MAGEE, D.D., afterwards Bishop of Peterborough preached to many crowded congregations.
		4. Sir WILLIAM HERSCHEL, astronomer and discoverer of the planet Uranus was organist at the Chapel from 1767 until he left the city.
31	LANSDOWN CRESCENT	1. JOHN PALMER built Lansdown Crescent 1789–92. As well as St James's Square and St Swithin's Church he was also responsible for completing the building of the original Orchard Street Theatre at Bath after the death of JOHN HIPPISLEY, a London actor of note, who first projected the idea in association with a Mr Watts. Mr Hippisley was also concerned in the theatre at JACOB'S WELLS in BRISTOL. The ORCHARD STREET THEATRE in BATH was opened in 1750 and many famous personalities appeared there including Mrs SIDDONS, Miss KEMBLE, SAMUEL FOOTE, HENDERSON and Mrs FARREN. JOHN PALMER, in 1768, obtained the first letters patent for any theatre in England for the enlarged Orchard Street building. This enabled him to use the title of 'THEATRE ROYAL'. He was also the originator of the Mail Coach, the cross-country system of transmitting mail.

LANSDOWN CRESCENT (Cont)

2. MISS IRVINE lived at No. 19 and many invitations to tea there were readily accepted by JANE AUSTEN. Jane who was born in 1775 spent many years living in or visiting Bath. Her novels were largely founded on Bath Society of the day and several were written in the city which will always be regarded as her spiritual home.

   It is interesting to reflect that when she was alive she had great difficulty in getting her books published and the fate which befell NORTHANGER ABBEY is a good illustration of this. She finished it in 1798 and eventually sold the manuscript for £10 in 1803 to Lewis Bull, a bookseller on the 'Lower Walks' (now Terrace Walk). Bull was the founder of a well-known library in Bond Street, London. After purchasing the book he apparently came to the conclusion that he had made a bad bargain and decided not to risk more money by printing. The manuscript thus lay on his shelves for many years until one of her brothers, induced by her progress elsewhere, called on the Bath publisher and negotiated the repurchase of the manuscript for the original sum of £10. Mr Bull was delighted to get his money back and Jane to recover her manuscript. Its later fame is well known and Mr Bull's thoughts may be well imagined.

   Jane died in 1817 and her enduring reputation and acclaim would no doubt have given her much 'grave and quiet satisfaction'.

3. WILLIAM BECKFORD, politician, writer and eccentric builder of towers moved to Lansdown Crescent after being forced by misfortune to sell his fantastic residence at FONTHILL ABBEY. He moved into 19 and 20 Lansdown Crescent in 1823 and the archway between the two houses was used as an extension to his immense library. He built his strange tower on Lansdown Hill which is now open to the public and a road from it passed through part garden and part wilderness adorned with temples and statues to an entrance in the back wall of his house in Lansdown Crescent. He lived in the Crescent until he died on May 2nd 1844, aged 84.

3 SALLY LUNN

1. SPRING GARDENS VAUXHALL were the very popular pleasure gardens situated on the East side of the river opposite the ORANGE GROVE. In summer months public breakfasts were held twice a week and in the evenings parties met to take tea. The proprietor was a Mr Purdie. There were many delightful, shady, walks. SALLY LUNNS were sold 'hot from the oven'.

2. Later known as TOMKINS FERRY BOAT (Tomkins was, unfortunately no relation to the author). The ferry was gaily decorated and plied regularly from 'Whitehall Stairs' across the river to Spring Gardens Vauxhall. It was often used by Elizabeth Linley and Sheridan. The stone steps can still be seen at the end of South Parade.

3. LILLIPUT ALLEY . . . Now also known as North Parade Passage.

4. DALMER was the enterprising baker-musician who saw the great possibilities of SALLY LUNNS. He bought the shop in Lilliput Alley and promoted sales on barrows around the town.

33	SALLY LUNN (Cont)	He also composed a song about SALLY LUNN which became a 'street favourite'. The shop, one of the oldest buildings in Bath, is still a popular meeting place and the 'Sally Lunns' served to customers are as popular as ever.
35	THE AMERICAN MUSEUM	1. THE MAYFLOWER — the historic ship used by the PILGRIM FATHERS on their voyage to New England. The American Museum was established in 1961 at CLAVERTON MANOR. It is the first American Museum ever to be opened outside the United States. It is furnished in authentic detail to give a vivid picture of American life from the 16th century until the Civil War.
37	THE CIRCUS	1. PHILLIP, second Earl Stanhope, lived at No. 5 from 1755 and was neighbour to the Right Hon. WILLIAM PITT at No. 7. There was a close intermarrying connection between the two families. The 3rd Earl married Lady Hester PITT, sister of William Pitt, and elder daughter of LORD CHATHAM. Their elder daughter was the well-known eccentric Lady HESTER LUCY STANHOPE. THOMAS GAINSBOROUGH the great portrait painter lived at No. 17. He came to BATH from Ipswich to be where the fashionable world resorted. At that time (1758) he painted three-quarter portraits at five guineas each in his rooms in the ABBEY CHURCHYARD. From there he moved to AINSLIE'S BELVEDERE and thence to THE CIRCUS when his success made a more imposing residence advisable. It was here that he produced some of his most famous works. His full length paintings rose in value from £50 to as much as £100 and his works here included the portraits of ELIZABETH LINLEY, RICHARD BRINSLEY SHERIDAN, LORD CHANCELLOR CAMDEN, JAMES QUIN (sometimes spelt QUINN), BURKE, GARRICK, STERNE, BISHOP HURD and many others. Today each would be worth a fortune.

37 THE CIRCUS (continued)

2. All 'sat' for Gainsborough.
3. DAVID GARRICK, actor. EDMUND BURKE, statesman (lived at 11 North Parade — as also did Oliver Goldsmith).
4. BISHOP RICHARD HURD, writer.
   JAMES QUIN, actor and wit, lived at 3a Pierrepoint Street.
   CHARLES PRATT, MARQUIS CAMDEN, politician and recorder of Bath.

41	No. 1 ROYAL CRESCENT	1. KING'S CIRCUS. Now known as The Circus. It was designed by the elder Wood and commenced in 1754. He laid the foundation stone shortly before his death in that year. Wood, the younger, saw the thirty houses of which it consists completed after the death of his father. The best known inhabitants of previous times have a bronze tablet to commemorate their residence.